Farm Animals

by Althea

pictures by Barbara McGirr

Published by Dinosaur Publications

Farmers choose the animals or crops which they enjoy or will do best on their land. This land gets too wet to grow some crops so a big herd of cattle is eating the grass growing there. Farm animals provide us with food and also with leather and wool.

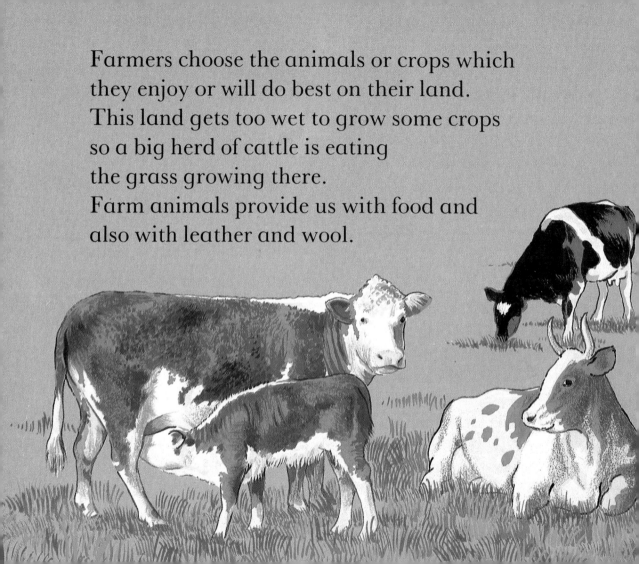

Cattle don't have top front teeth so
they wrap their tongues around the grass
and tear it off. The farmer cuts and stores
some of the grass to feed to the cattle
when they come inside for the winter.

These two-day-old calves have been taken away from their mothers. They quickly learn to drink milk from a bucket. Soon they will have solid food too.

Their mothers are producing milk for people to drink or for making into cheese or butter.

The cows are lining up, waiting
to be taken in for milking.
They are milked each morning
and evening.

They can have an extra ration of food at the same time. The blue box on their collars measures the ration they eat, so they can't eat too much.

Sheep can live and feed on rough grass.
The lambs are suckling milk from
their mothers. Soon they too will be
nibbling the grass.

Sheep are bred for their wool
and for meat.
Each year their thick fleece is cut off
in one piece and sold to make cloth
or knitting wool.

The sheepdog helps to round up
the sheep to take them in for
shearing or weighing.

Chickens are bred for their eggs or for meat. The lights stay on in this hen house for about sixteen hours a day to give them lots of time to eat, drink and lay eggs.

The goose sits on her eggs
to keep them warm.
The first eggs she laid this year
were taken to be eaten.
She is allowed to keep this clutch, which
will hatch into a family of goslings.

Bantam and duck eggs are good
to eat too.
These ducks don't fly. The bantams
and ducks must be shut up at night to
keep them safe from foxes.

Geese are good guards and will make
a lot of noise if they think there is
any danger.

Some pigs live outside but most live in special pig houses. The sow will have two litters or more of about ten piglets each year.
The piglets can run outside the farrowing crate, so the sow can't lie down on them by accident.

Pigs love acorns as a special treat,
they spit out the skins.
They are big eaters and drink
a lot of water.
Male pigs are called boars.
They can be very fierce.

Many people enjoy riding.
These horses have a donkey
to keep them company.
They flick their tails and
wiggle their ears to try to
stop flies settling on them.

Before tractors became common
heavy horses were used to pull ploughs
and till the land.
Now these working horses are kept
mainly for breeding
and showing.

This small farm has goats.
Their milk is used to make cheese and
yoghourt and is also good to drink.
Sheep are sometimes milked too.

The calf will be sold to
another farmer when she is two.
She will be old enough to have
a calf of her own and then start
producing milk.

The dog keeps guard and
the cats catch rats and mice.

Some exotic breeds of animal are kept
to save them from becoming extinct.
They are shown at county shows or at
farms that are open to the public.

Animals in city farms are very tame. Families and school parties can learn more about the animals and even help to look after them.

They have horses too, which people can hire and learn to ride.

But most farms have to be run
like a business to make money.
They grow the crops or rear the animals
to provide the food we like to eat.

The main difficulty is to decide how
much of one sort of food people will
want so it is not wasted.
When the weather is good,
surplus food is often produced.
More planning is needed to get extra food
to the people who need it around the world.

Text copyright © Althea Braithwaite 1986
Illustrations copyright © Barbara McGirr 1986
Published by Dinosaur Publications
8 Grafton Street
London W1X 3LA

Dinosaur Publications is an imprint
of Fontana Paperbacks, a division
of the Collins Publishing Group
Printed by Warners of Bourne and London